Orange Juice

BEFORE THE STORE

BY RYAN JACOBSON · ILLUSTRATED BY DAN McGEEHAN

Published by The Child's World®
1980 Lookout Drive • Mankato, MN 56003-1705
800-599-READ • www.childsworld.com

ACKNOWLEDGMENTS
The Child's World®: Mary Berendes, Publishing Director
The Design Lab: Design and production
Red Line Editorial: Editorial direction
Content Consultant: Kyle W. Stiegert, Professor and Director of Food System Research Group,
    University of Wisconsin-Madison

ISBN 9781609736781
LCCN 2011940074

PHOTO CREDITS
Dreamstime, cover (background); Inacio Pires/Shutterstock Images, cover (inset); Shutterstock Images,
5, 17, 21, 30 (middle); Jason Patrick Ross/Shutterstock Images, 7; Tono Balaguer/Bigstock, 9, 30 (top);
Fotolia, 13, 30 (bottom); Yali Shi/Dreamstime, 27; Sean Locke/iStockphoto, 29, 31 (top)

Design elements: Dreamstime

Printed in the United States of America

ABOUT THE AUTHOR

Ryan Jacobson is the author of nearly 20 books, including picture books, chapter books, graphic novels, choose-your-path books, and ghost stories. He lives in Mora, Minnesota, with his wife Lora, sons Jonah and Lucas, and dog Boo.

Contents

CHAPTER ONE

Sweet Orange Juice

Orange juice is sweet and a little sour. It is healthy, too. And it is not just for breakfast. People drink orange juice any time of day. When do you drink orange juice?

Orange juice comes from oranges. But have you ever wondered how orange juice is made? There are many steps. The first step starts at orange farms. That is where oranges are grown.

Orange juice is great for breakfast.

CHAPTER TWO

At the Orange Farm

Oranges grow on trees. They need plenty of rain and sunshine. Florida is one of the best places for oranges to grow. Most oranges in the United States are grown in Florida. And most oranges grow on orange farms.

Orange farms have hundreds or thousands of orange trees. The trees are planted in groups called groves. People like to drink orange juice all year long. So orange farmers grow several different kinds of oranges. Some are sold as whole fruit, but most are

Oranges for orange juice are grown on farms.

made into juice. The different kinds become ripe at different times of year. You can buy fresh oranges most months of the year.

A crew of pickers goes into the groves when the oranges are ripe. This group of people pulls the fruit off the trees. The picked oranges are sent to a packing center. Some of the fruit is boxed for sale. The rest is loaded into large trucks. The trucks haul the oranges to orange juice factories.

The oranges that are grown in Florida include Navel, Hamlin, Pineapple, Amber-sweet, and Valencia.

Pickers grab ripe oranges from the trees.

CHAPTER THREE

To the Orange Juice Factory

When the oranges arrive at the factory, they are tested. An inspector tests a **sample** of them. Each sample weighs about 40 pounds (18 kg). The tests show if the oranges are ripe and safe to eat. Oranges that pass the tests are washed. A special soap is used. Then the oranges are rinsed with water. Any

> Oranges are ripe when their water content is 10 percent sugar.

Oranges are washed in a machine.

insects or dirt are washed away. Next the fruit is dried. Now the oranges move on a **conveyer belt** and are taken through a machine. The machine removes twigs and leaves from the oranges.

Next a group of workers **grade** the oranges. The workers inspect the oranges by hand. They remove oranges that do not have an orange color. If an orange looks green, it is not ripe. If an orange has dark spots, it is rotten. Then the fruit is separated by size in a machine.

The fruit is inspected so that only good fruit is squeezed for juice.

Now the oranges can be made into juice. The conveyer belt carries the oranges to a machine. It is the juice **extractor**. Different juice extractors work in different ways. Some poke holes into the oranges. Others cut them in half. But all squeeze the juice out of every orange. While this happens, the peels are sliced away. The peels are removed from the machine. But the peels are not all thrown away. Some are fed to cattle.

The juice next falls through a screen. The screen takes out any chunks of fruit. Pure, smooth orange juice is all that is left.

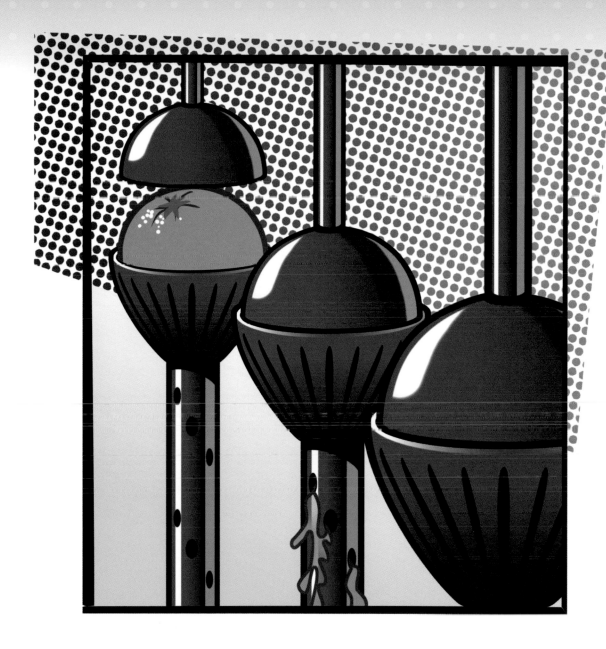

Oranges are juiced in a juice extractor.

CHAPTER FOUR

Kinds of Juice

Some orange juice is pure liquid. Other orange juice comes mixed with **pulp**. Pulp is small bits of orange fruit. All of the pulp is taken out when orange juice is made. The juice is divided into batches. Some batches get mixed with pulp. If it is "high pulp" juice, a lot of pulp is mixed in. If it is "low pulp" juice, less pulp gets mixed in. If it is "no pulp" juice, pulp does not get added at all.

Pulp comes from the inside part of oranges.

Much of the orange juice we buy is **concentrated**.
Water was taken out of the juice. A special machine
uses steam to heat the juice. It makes the water
evaporate out of the juice. Concentrated juice takes
up less space in a warehouse. It also weighs less. And it
makes the juice last longer than fresh juice.

The juice is heated in a tub.

To drink concentrated juice, we must mix in water. If your family buys frozen orange juice, you mix it with water at home. Orange juice in a carton has been mixed or was never concentrated.

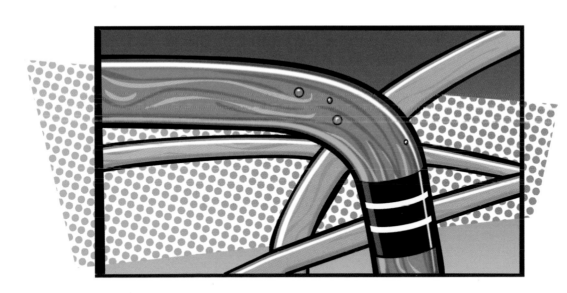

The concentrate moves through pipes in a factory.

Orange juice is filled with Vitamin C. This vitamin helps your bones, teeth, and skin stay healthy and grow.

Not all orange juice is just juice. Some extra **ingredients** might be added. **Preservatives** keep the orange juice fresher for longer. Sweeteners such as honey or sugar may be mixed in. Flavor packets might be included to make the juice taste fresh. Or citric acid may be added to make it taste tart. Some orange juices have calcium added.

Honey is sometimes added to orange juice.

Some orange juice is mixed with other juices to make a juice blend. Strawberry and pineapple juice taste great when mixed with orange juice!

You can drink fresh orange juice right away. But it does not stay fresh for long. It is next **pasteurized**. The juice is heated in a machine. This machine kills **bacteria**. Some bacteria can make people sick. This step makes orange juice safe to drink for months.

Pasteurized juice has been heated to kill bacteria.

CHAPTER FIVE

Into the Containers

Orange juice next needs to be put into cartons or bottles. A conveyor belt brings cartons and bottles to a filling machine. Juice pours into the machine from giant storage tanks. The machine pours the right amount of juice into each carton or bottle.

The containers are next sealed by another machine. The containers go under a special printer. It labels them with the date the juice **expires**. Then the containers are quickly cooled.

A machine fills cartons with juice.

This is the last step. The orange juice inside should last for up to eight months!

It takes 18 oranges to make one half-gallon (2 L) carton of orange juice!

The cartons and bottles are wrapped in plastic for shipping. They are ready to be loaded onto trucks and shipped away from the factory.

Bottles are sealed and cooled before they go to the store.

CHAPTER SIX

Into Your Glass

The orange juice is loaded into refrigerated trucks. The containers are shipped to grocery stores, gas stations, and other places that sell orange juice. Most of the juice is kept cool in a store refrigerator. Some of the concentrated juice can be found in the freezer aisle. And some juice sits on shelves. It does not need to be kept cold.

Now it is your turn! You can pick your favorite kind of orange juice. Will it have lots of pulp, a little

pulp, or none at all? You can also choose a blend.
And how will you drink your orange juice? Try it in
an orange and banana smoothie. Enjoy!

You can find orange juice at a grocery store.

ORANGE JUICE MAP

1

ORANGES PICKED AT THE FARM

2

WASHED AND GRADED

3

PULP ADDED

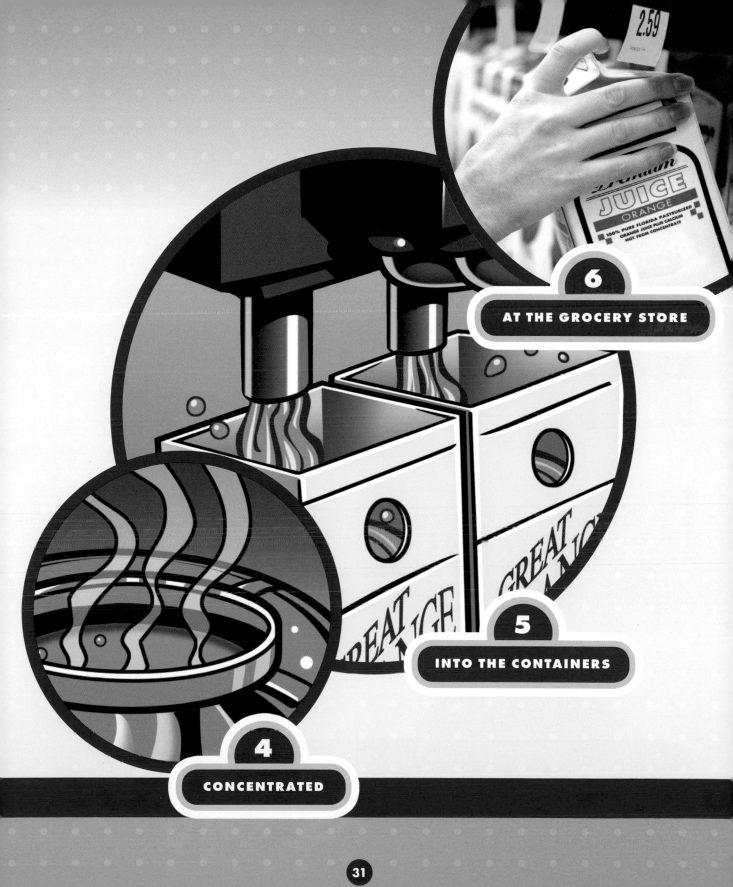

6 AT THE GROCERY STORE

JUICE
ORANGE
100% PURE FLORIDA PASTEURIZED
ORANGE JUICE PLUS CALCIUM
NOT FROM CONCENTRATE

5 INTO THE CONTAINERS

4 CONCENTRATED

bacteria (bak-TIHR-ee-uh): Bacteria are small living things that are harmful or helpful. Orange juice is pasteurized to kill bacteria in the juice.

concentrated (KON-suhn-trate-ed): A concentrated liquid is one that has been made thicker and stronger tasting by removing water from it. Most juice is concentrated.

conveyor belt (kuhn-VAY-ur BELT): A conveyor belt is a moving belt that takes materials from one place to another in a factory. Orange juice containers move on a conveyor belt in the factory.

evaporate (i-VAP-uh-rate): To evaporate is when liquid turns into a gas. Water will evaporate when juice is heated.

expires (ek-SPIREZ): Something expires when it reaches the end of the time it can be used. Orange juice expires after a certain time.

extractor (ek-STRAKT-or): An extractor is a machine that pulls something out, such as juice from an orange. A juice extractor is used to make orange juice.

grade (grayd): To grade is to judge the quality of something. Workers grade oranges in the factory.

ingredients (in-GREE-dee-uhnts): Ingredients are things that are added to a mixture, like items in a recipe list. Other ingredients can be added to orange juice.

pasteurized (PASS-chuh-rized): Food is pasteurized when it is heated to a high temperature and harmful bacteria is killed. Orange juice needs to be pasteurized.

preservatives (pri-ZUR-vuh-tivz): Preservatives are chemicals added to foods and drinks to keep them from spoiling. Some kinds of orange juice contain preservatives.

pulp (puhlp): Pulp is the soft, juicy flesh parts of fruit. Pulp is added to some kinds of orange juice.

sample (SAM-puhl): A sample is a small part of something that shows what the whole of something is like. A sample of the oranges are tested.

Mayo, Gretchen Will. *Orange Juice*. Milwaukee, WI: Weekly Reader Early Learning Library, 2004.

Rosenberg, Pam. *Orange Juice: How Did That Get to My Table?* Ann Arbor, MI: Cherry Lake Publishing, 2010.

Snyder, Inez. *Oranges to Orange Juice*. New York: Children's Press, 2003.

Visit our Web site for links about orange juice production: childsworld.com/links

Note to Parents, Teachers, and Librarians: We routinely verify our Web links to make sure they are safe and active sites. So encourage your readers to check them out!